THE SOLID FACTS

SECOND EDITION

Edited by Richard Wilkinson and Michael Marmot

WHO Library Cataloguing in Publication Data

Social determinants of health: the solid facts. 2nd edition / edited by
Richard Wilkinson and Michael Marmot.

  1.Socioeconomic factors 2.Social environment 3.Social support
  4.Health behavior 5.Health status 6.Public health 7.Health promotion
  8.Europe I.Wilkinson, Richard II.Marmot, Michael.

  ISBN 92 890 1371 0   (NLM Classification : WA 30)

Address requests about publications of the WHO Regional Office to:

• by e-mail publicationrequests@euro.who.int (for copies of publications)
          permissions@euro.who.int (for permission to reproduce them)
          pubrights@euro.who.int (for permission to translate them)

• by post   Publications
          WHO Regional Office for Europe
          Scherfigsvej 8
          DK-2100 Copenhagen Ø, Denmark

ISBN 92 890 1371 0

CONTENTS

The World Health Organization was established in 1948 as a specialized agency of the United Nations serving as the directing and coordinating authority for international health matters and public health. One of WHO's constitutional functions is to provide objective and reliable information and advice in the field of human health, a responsibility that it fulfils in part through its publications programmes. Through its publications, the Organization seeks to support national health strategies and address the most pressing public health concerns.

The WHO Regional Office for Europe is one of six regional offices throughout the world, each with its own programme geared to the particular health problems of the countries it serves. The European Region embraces some 870 million people living in an area stretching from Greenland in the north and the Mediterranean in the south to the Pacific shores of the Russian Federation. The European programme of WHO therefore concentrates both on the problems associated with industrial and post-industrial society and on those faced by the emerging democracies of central and eastern Europe and the former USSR.

To ensure the widest possible availability of authoritative information and guidance on health matters, WHO secures broad international distribution of its publications and encourages their translation and adaptation. By helping to promote and protect health and prevent and control disease, WHO's books contribute to achieving the Organization's principal objective – the attainment by all people of the highest possible level of health.

WHO Centre for Urban Health

This publication is an initiative of the Centre for Urban Health, at the WHO Regional Office for Europe. The technical focus of the work of the Centre is on developing tools and resource materials in the areas of health policy, integrated planning for health and sustainable development, urban planning, governance and social support. The Centre is responsible for the Healthy Cities and urban governance programme.

The need and demand for clear scientific evidence to inform and support the health policy-making process are greater than ever. The field of the social determinants of health is perhaps the most complex and challenging of all. It is concerned with key aspects of people's living and working circumstances and with their lifestyles. It is concerned with the health implications of economic and social policies, as well as with the benefits that investing in health policies can bring. In the past five years, since the publication of the first edition of Social determinants of health. The solid facts *in 1998, new and stronger scientific evidence has been developed. This second edition integrates the new evidence and is enriched with graphs, further reading and recommended web sites.*

Our goal is to promote awareness, informed debate and, above all, action. We want to build on the success of the first edition, which was translated into 25 languages and used by decision-makers at all levels, public health professionals and academics throughout the European Region and beyond. The good news is that an increasing number of Member States today are developing policies and programmes that explicitly address the root causes of ill health, health inequalities and the needs of those who are affected by poverty and social disadvantage.

This publication was achieved through close partnership between the WHO Centre for Urban Health and the International Centre for Health and Society, University College London, United Kingdom. I should like to express my gratitude to Professor Richard Wilkinson and Professor Sir Michael Marmot, who edited the publication, and to thank all the members of the scientific team who contributed to this important piece of work. I am convinced that it will be a valuable tool for broadening the understanding of and stimulating debate and action on the social determinants of health.

Agis D. Tsouros

Head, Centre for Urban Health
WHO Regional Office for Europe

Professor Mel Bartley, University College London, United Kingdom

Dr David Blane, Imperial College London, United Kingdom

Dr Eric Brunner, International Centre for Health and Society, University College London, United Kingdom

Professor Danny Dorling, School of Geography, University of Leeds, United Kingdom

Dr Jane Ferrie, University College London, United Kingdom

Professor Martin Jarvis, Cancer Research UK, Health Behaviour Unit, University College London, United Kingdom

Professor Sir Michael Marmot, Department of Epidemiology and Public Health and International Centre for Health and Society, University College London, United Kingdom

Professor Mark McCarthy, University College London, United Kingdom

Dr Mary Shaw, Department of Social Medicine, Bristol University, United Kingdom

Professor Aubrey Sheiham, International Centre for Health and Society, University College London, United Kingdom

Professor Stephen Stansfeld, Barts and The London, Queen Mary's School of Medicine and Dentistry, London

Professor Mike Wadsworth, Medical Research Council, National Survey of Health and Development, University College London, United Kingdom

Professor Richard Wilkinson, University of Nottingham, United Kingdom

Even in the most affluent countries, people who are less well off have substantially shorter life expectancies and more illnesses than the rich. Not only are these differences in health an important social injustice, they have also drawn scientific attention to some of the most powerful determinants of health standards in modern societies. They have led in particular to a growing understanding of the remarkable sensitivity of health to the social environment and to what have become known as the social determinants of health.

This publication outlines the most important parts of this new knowledge as it relates to areas of public policy. The ten topics covered include the lifelong importance of health determinants in early childhood, and the effects of poverty, drugs, working conditions, unemployment, social support, good food and transport policy. To provide the background, we start with a discussion of the social gradient in health, followed by an explanation of how psychological and social influences affect physical health and longevity.

In each case, the focus is on the role that public policy can play in shaping the social environment in ways conducive to better health: that focus is maintained whether we are looking at behavioural factors, such as the quality of parenting, nutrition, exercise and substance abuse, or at more structural issues such as unemployment, poverty and the experience of work. Each of the chapters contains a brief summary of what has been most reliably established by research, followed by a list of implications for public policy. A few key references to the research are listed at the end of each chapter, but a fuller discussion of the evidence

can be found in *Social determinants of health* (Marmot M, Wilkinson RG, eds. Oxford, Oxford University Press, 1999), which was prepared to accompany the first edition of *Social determinants of health. The solid facts*. For both publications, we are indebted to researchers in the forefront of their fields, most of whom are associated with the International Centre for Health and Society at University College London. They have given their time and expertise to draft the different chapters of both these publications.

Health policy was once thought to be about little more than the provision and funding of medical care: the social determinants of health were discussed only among academics. This is now changing. While medical care can prolong survival and improve prognosis after some serious diseases, more important for the health of the population as a whole are the social and economic conditions that make people ill and in need of medical care in the first place. Nevertheless, universal access to medical care is clearly one of the social determinants of health.

Why also, in a new publication on the determinants of health, is there nothing about genes? The new discoveries on the human genome are exciting in the promise they hold for advances in the understanding and treatment of specific diseases. But however important *individual* genetic susceptibilities to disease may be, the common causes of the ill health that affects *populations* are environmental: they come and go far more quickly than the slow pace of genetic change because they reflect the changes in the way we live. This is why life expectancy has improved so dramatically over recent generations; it is also why some European

People's lifestyles and the conditions in which they live and work strongly influence their health.

countries have improved their health while others have not, and it is why health differences between different social groups have widened or narrowed as social and economic conditions have changed.

The evidence on which this publication is based comes from very large numbers of research reports – many thousands in all. Some of the studies have used prospective methods, sometimes following tens of thousands of people over decades – sometimes from birth. Others have used cross-sectional methods and have studied individual, area, national or international data. Difficulties that have sometimes arisen (perhaps despite follow-up studies) in determining causality have been overcome by using evidence from intervention studies, from so-called natural experiments, and occasionally from studies of other primate species. Nevertheless, as both health and the major influences on it vary substantially according to levels of economic development, the reader should keep in mind that the bulk of the evidence on which this publication is based comes from rich developed countries and its relevance to less developed countries may be limited.

Our intention has been to ensure that policy at all levels – in government, public and private institutions, workplaces and the community – takes proper account of recent evidence suggesting a wider responsibility for creating healthy societies. But a publication as short as this cannot provide a comprehensive guide to determinants of public health. Several areas of health policy, such as the need to safeguard people from exposure to toxic materials at work, are left out because they are well known (though often not adequately enforced). As exhortations to individual behaviour change are also a well established approach to health promotion, and the evidence suggests they may sometimes have limited effect, there is little about what individuals can do to improve their own health. We do, however, emphasize the need to understand how behaviour is shaped by the environment and, consistent with approaching health through its social determinants, recommend environmental changes that would lead to healthier behaviour.

Given that this publication was put together from the contributions of acknowledged experts in each field, what is striking is the extent to which the sections converge on the need for a more just and caring society – both economically and socially. Combining economics, sociology and psychology with neurobiology and medicine, it looks as if much depends on understanding the interaction between material disadvantage and its social meanings. It is not simply that poor material circumstances are harmful to health; the social meaning of being poor, unemployed, socially excluded, or otherwise stigmatized also matters. As social beings, we need not only good material conditions but, from early childhood onwards, we need to feel valued and appreciated. We need friends, we need more sociable societies, we need to feel useful, and we need to exercise a significant degree of control over meaningful work. Without these we become more prone to depression, drug use, anxiety, hostility and feelings of hopelessness, which all rebound on physical health.

We hope that by tackling some of the material and social injustices, policy will not only improve health and well-being, but may also reduce a range of other social problems that flourish alongside ill health and are rooted in some of the same socioeconomic processes.

Richard Wilkinson and Michael Marmot

Life expectancy is shorter and most diseases are more common further down the social ladder in each society. Health policy must tackle the social and economic determinants of health.

What is known

Poor social and economic circumstances affect health throughout life. People further down the social ladder usually run at least twice the risk of serious illness and premature death as those near the top. Nor are the effects confined to the poor: the social gradient in health runs right across society, so that even among middle-class office workers, lower ranking staff suffer much more disease and earlier death than higher ranking staff (Fig. 1).

Fig. 1. Occupational class differences in life expectancy, England and Wales, 1997–1999

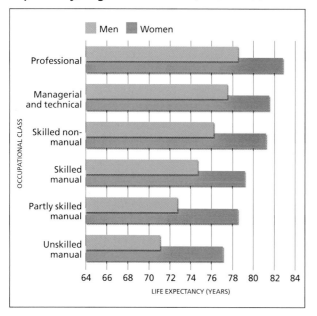

Both material and psychosocial causes contribute to these differences and their effects extend to most diseases and causes of death.

Disadvantage has many forms and may be absolute or relative. It can include having few family assets, having a poorer education during adolescence, having insecure employment, becoming stuck in a hazardous or dead-end job, living in poor housing, trying to bring up a family in difficult circumstances and living on an inadequate retirement pension.

These disadvantages tend to concentrate among the same people, and their effects on health accumulate during life. The longer people live in stressful economic and social circumstances, the greater the physiological wear and tear they suffer, and the less likely they are to enjoy a healthy old age.

Policy implications

If policy fails to address these facts, it not only ignores the most powerful determinants of health standards in modern societies, it also ignores one of the most important social justice issues facing modern societies.

- Life contains a series of critical transitions: emotional and material changes in early childhood, the move from primary to secondary education, starting work, leaving home and starting a family, changing jobs and facing possible redundancy, and eventually retirement. Each of these changes can affect health by pushing people onto a more or less advantaged path. Because people who have been disadvantaged in the past are at the greatest risk in each subsequent transition, welfare policies need to provide not only safety nets but also springboards to offset earlier disadvantage.

- Good health involves reducing levels of educational failure, reducing insecurity and unemployment and improving housing standards. Societies that enable all citizens to play a full and useful role in the social, economic and cultural life of their society will be healthier than those where people face insecurity, exclusion and deprivation.

- Other chapters of this publication cover specific policy areas and suggest ways of improving health that will also reduce the social gradient in health.

Poor social and economic circumstances affect health throughout life.

KEY SOURCES

Bartley M, Plewis I. Accumulated labour market disadvantage and limiting long-term illness. *International Journal of Epidemiology,* 2002, 31:336–341.

Mitchell R, Blane D, Bartley M. Elevated risk of high blood pressure: climate and the inverse housing law. *International Journal of Epidemiology,* 2002, 31:831–838.

Montgomery SM, Berney LR, Blane D. Prepubertal stature and blood pressure in early old age. *Archives of Disease in Childhood,* 2000, 82:358–363.

Morris JN et al. A minimum income for healthy living. *Journal of Epidemiology and Community Health,* 2000, 54:885–889.

Programme Committee on Socio-economic Inequalities in Health (SEGV-II). *Reducing socio-economic inequalities in health.* The Hague, Ministry of Health, Welfare and Sport, 2001.

van de Mheen H et al. Role of childhood health in the explanation of socioeconomic inequalities in early adult health. *Journal of Epidemiology and Community Health,* 1998, 52:15–19.

Source of Fig. 1: Donkin A, Goldblatt P, Lynch K. Inequalities in life expectancy by social class 1972–1999. *Health Statistics Quarterly,* 2002, 15:5–15.

Stressful circumstances, making people feel worried, anxious and unable to cope, are damaging to health and may lead to premature death.

What is known

Social and psychological circumstances can cause long-term stress. Continuing anxiety, insecurity, low self-esteem, social isolation and lack of control over work and home life, have powerful effects on health. Such psychosocial risks accumulate during life and increase the chances of poor mental health and premature death. Long periods of anxiety and insecurity and the lack of supportive friendships are damaging in whatever area of life they arise. The lower people are in the social hierarchy of industrialized countries, the more common these problems become.

Why do these psychosocial factors affect physical health? In emergencies, our hormones and nervous system prepare us to deal with an immediate physical threat by triggering the fight or flight response: raising the heart rate, mobilizing stored energy, diverting blood to muscles and increasing alertness. Although the stresses of modern urban life rarely demand strenuous or even moderate

Lack of control over work and home can have powerful effects on health.

© RIKKE STEENVINKEL NORDENHOF/POLFOTO

physical activity, turning on the stress response diverts energy and resources away from many physiological processes important to long-term health maintenance. Both the cardiovascular and immune systems are affected. For brief periods, this does not matter; but if people feel tense too often or the tension goes on for too long, they become more vulnerable to a wide range of conditions including infections, diabetes, high blood pressure, heart attack, stroke, depression and aggression.

KEY SOURCES

Brunner EJ. Stress and the biology of inequality. *British Medical Journal,* 1997, 314:1472–1476.

Brunner EJ et al. Adrenocortical, autonomic and inflammatory causes of the metabolic syndrome. *Circulation,* 2002, 106: 2659–2665.

Kivimaki M et al. Work stress and risk of cardiovascular mortality: prospective cohort study of industrial employees. *British Medical Journal,* 2002, 325:857–860.

Marmot MG, Stansfeld SA. *Stress and heart disease.* London, BMJ Books, 2002.

Marmot MG et al. Contribution of job control and other risk factors to social variations in coronary heart disease incidence. *Lancet,* 1997, 350:235–239.

Policy implications

Although a medical response to the biological changes that come with stress may be to try to control them with drugs, attention should be focused upstream, on reducing the major causes of chronic stress.

- In schools, workplaces and other institutions, the quality of the social environment and material security are often as important to health as the physical environment. Institutions that can give people a sense of belonging, participating and being valued are likely to be healthier places than those where people feel excluded, disregarded and used.

- Governments should recognize that welfare programmes need to address both psychosocial and material needs: both are sources of anxiety and insecurity. In particular, governments should support families with young children, encourage community activity, combat social isolation, reduce material and financial insecurity, and promote coping skills in education and rehabilitation.

A good start in life means supporting mothers and young children: the health impact of early development and education lasts a lifetime.

What is known

Observational research and intervention studies show that the foundations of adult health are laid in early childhood and before birth. Slow growth and poor emotional support raise the lifetime risk of poor physical health and reduce physical, cognitive and emotional functioning in adulthood. Poor early experience and slow growth become embedded in biology during the processes of development, and form the basis of the individual's biological and human capital, which affects health throughout life.

Poor circumstances during pregnancy can lead to less than optimal fetal development via a chain that may include deficiencies in nutrition during pregnancy, maternal stress, a greater likelihood of maternal smoking and misuse of drugs and alcohol, insufficient exercise and inadequate prenatal care. Poor fetal development is a risk for health in later life (Fig. 2).

Infant experience is important to later

health because of the continued malleability of biological systems. As cognitive, emotional and sensory inputs programme the brain's responses, insecure emotional attachment and poor stimulation can lead to reduced readiness for school, low educational attainment, and problem behaviour, and the risk of social marginalization in adulthood. Good health-related habits, such as eating sensibly, exercising and not smoking, are associated with parental and peer group examples, and with good education. Slow or retarded physical growth in infancy is associated with reduced cardiovascular, respiratory, pancreatic and kidney development and function, which increase the risk of illness in adulthood.

© FINN FRANDSEN/POLFOTO

Important foundations of adult health are laid in early childhood.

Fig. 2. Risk of diabetes in men aged 64 years by birth weight

Adjusted for body mass index

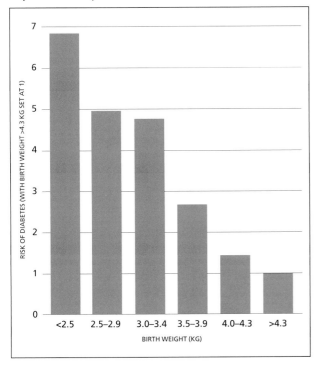

Policies for improving health in early life should aim to:

- increase the general level of education and provide equal opportunity of access to education, to improve the health of mothers and babies in the long run;

- provide good nutrition, health education, and health and preventive care facilities, and adequate social and economic resources, before first pregnancies, during pregnancy, and in infancy, to improve growth and development before birth and throughout infancy, and reduce the risk of disease and malnutrition in infancy; and

- ensure that parent–child relations are supported from birth, ideally through home visiting and the encouragement of good parental relations with schools, to increase parental knowledge of children's emotional and cognitive needs, to stimulate cognitive development and pro-social behaviour in the child, and to prevent child abuse.

Policy implications

These risks to the developing child are significantly greater among those in poor socioeconomic circumstances, and they can best be reduced through improved preventive health care before the first pregnancy and for mothers and babies in pre- and postnatal, infant welfare and school clinics, and through improvements in the educational levels of parents and children. Such health and education programmes have direct benefits. They increase parents' awareness of their children's needs and their receptivity to information about health and development, and they increase parental confidence in their own effectiveness.

KEY SOURCES

Barker DJP. *Mothers, babies and disease in later life,* 2nd ed. Edinburgh, Churchill Livingstone, 1998.

Keating DP, Hertzman C, eds. *Developmental health and the wealth of nations.* New York, NY, Guilford Press, 1999.

Mehrotra S, Jolly R, eds. *Development with a human face.* Oxford, Oxford University Press, 2000.

Rutter M, Rutter M. *Developing minds: challenge and continuity across the life span.* London, Penguin Books, 1993.

Wallace HM, Giri K, Serrano CV, eds. *Health care of women and children in developing countries,* 2nd ed. Santa Monica, CA, Third Party Publishing, 1995.

Source of Fig. 2: Barker DJP. *Mothers, babies and disease in later life,* 2nd ed. Edinburgh, Churchill Livingstone, 1998.

Life is short where its quality is poor. By causing hardship and resentment, poverty, social exclusion and discrimination cost lives.

What is known

Poverty, relative deprivation and social exclusion have a major impact on health and premature death, and the chances of living in poverty are loaded heavily against some social groups.

Absolute poverty – a lack of the basic material necessities of life – continues to exist, even in the richest countries of Europe. The unemployed, many ethnic minority groups, guest workers, disabled people, refugees and homeless people are at particular risk. Those living on the streets suffer the highest rates of premature death.

Relative poverty means being much poorer than most people in society and is often defined as living on less than 60% of the national median income. It denies people access to decent housing, education, transport and other factors vital to full participation in life. Being excluded from the life of society and treated as less than equal leads to worse health and greater risks of premature death. The stresses of living in poverty are particularly harmful during pregnancy, to babies, children and old people. In some countries, as much as one quarter of the total population – and a higher proportion of children – live in relative poverty (Fig. 3).

Social exclusion also results from racism, discrimination, stigmatization, hostility and unemployment. These processes prevent people from participating in education or training, and gaining access to services and citizenship activities. They are socially and psychologically damaging, materially costly, and harmful to health. People who live in, or have left, institutions, such as prisons, children's homes and psychiatric hospitals, are particularly vulnerable.

The greater the length of time that people live in disadvantaged circumstances, the more likely they are to suffer from a range of health problems, particularly cardiovascular disease. People move in and out of poverty during their lives, so the number of people who experience poverty and social exclusion during their lifetime is far higher than the current number of socially excluded people.

Poverty and social exclusion increase the risks of divorce and separation, disability, illness, addiction and social isolation and

People living on the streets suffer the highest rates of premature death.

© JAN GRARUP/POLFOTO

Fig. 3. Proportion of children living in poor households (below 50% of the national average income)

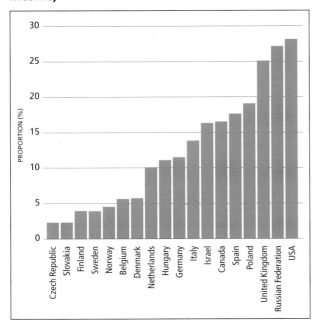

vice versa, forming vicious circles that deepen the predicament people face.

As well as the direct effects of being poor, health can also be compromised indirectly by living in neighbourhoods blighted by concentrations of deprivation, high unemployment, poor quality housing, limited access to services and a poor quality environment.

Policy implications

Through policies on taxes, benefits, employment, education, economic management, and many other areas of activity, no government can avoid having a major impact on the distribution of income. The indisputable evidence of the effects of such policies on rates of death and disease imposes a public duty to eliminate absolute poverty and reduce material inequalities.

- All citizens should be protected by minimum income guarantees, minimum wages legislation and access to services.

- Interventions to reduce poverty and social exclusion are needed at both the individual and the neighbourhood levels.

- Legislation can help protect minority and vulnerable groups from discrimination and social exclusion.

- Public health policies should remove barriers to health care, social services and affordable housing.

- Labour market, education and family welfare policies should aim to reduce social stratification.

KEY SOURCES

Claussen B, Davey Smith G, Thelle D. Impact of childhood and adulthood socio-economic position on cause specific mortality: the Oslo Mortality Study. *Journal of Epidemiology and Community Health,* 2003, 57:40–45.

Kawachi I, Berkman L, eds. *Neighborhoods and health.* Oxford, Oxford University Press, 2003.

Mackenbach J, Bakker M, eds. *Reducing inequalities in health: a European perspective.* London, Routledge, 2002.

Shaw M, Dorling D, Brimblecombe N. Life chances in Britain by housing wealth and for the homeless and vulnerably housed. *Environment and Planning A,*1999, 31:2239–2248.

Townsend P, Gordon D. *World poverty: new policies to defeat an old enemy.* Bristol, The Policy Press, 2002.

Source of Fig. 3: Bradshaw J. Child poverty in comparative perspective. In: Gordon D, Townsend P. *Breadline Europe: the measurement of poverty.* Bristol, The Policy Press, 2000.

Stress in the workplace increases the risk of disease. People who have more control over their work have better health.

What is known

In general, having a job is better for health than having no job. But the social organization of work, management styles and social relationships in the workplace all matter for health. Evidence shows that stress at work plays an important role in contributing to the large social status differences in health, sickness absence and premature death. Several European workplace studies show that health suffers when people have little opportunity to use their skills and low decision-making authority.

Fig. 4. Self-reported level of job control and incidence of coronary heart disease in men and women

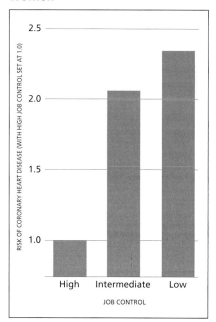

Adjusted for age, sex, length of follow-up, effort/reward imbalance, employment grade, coronary risk factors and negative psychological disposition

Having little control over one's work is particularly strongly related to an increased risk of low back pain, sickness absence and cardiovascular disease (Fig. 4). These risks have been found to be independent of the psychological characteristics of the people studied. In short, they seem to be related to the work environment.

Studies have also examined the role of work demands. Some show an interaction between demands and control. Jobs with both high demand and low control carry special risk. Some evidence indicates that social support in the workplace may be protective.

Further, receiving inadequate rewards for the effort put into work has been found to be associated with increased cardiovascular risk. Rewards can take the form of money, status and self-esteem. Current changes in the labour market may change the opportunity structure, and make it harder for people to get appropriate rewards.

These results show that the psychosocial environment at work is an important determinant of health and contributor to the social gradient in ill health.

Policy implications

- There is no trade-off between health and productivity at work. A virtuous circle can be established: improved conditions of work will lead to a healthier work force, which will lead to improved productivity, and hence to the opportunity to create a still healthier, more productive workplace.

- Appropriate involvement in decision-making is likely to benefit employees at all levels of an organization. Mechanisms should therefore be developed to allow people to influence the design and improvement of their work environment, thus enabling employees to have more control, greater variety and more opportunities for development at work.

- Good management involves ensuring appropriate rewards – in terms of money, status and self-esteem – for all employees.

- To reduce the burden of musculoskeletal disorders, workplaces must be ergonomically appropriate.

- As well as requiring an effective infrastructure with legal controls and powers of inspection, workplace health protection should also include workplace health services with people trained in the early detection of mental health problems and appropriate interventions.

Jobs with both high demand and low control carry special risk.

© FIRST LIGHT

KEY SOURCES

Bosma H et al. Two alternative job stress models and risk of coronary heart disease. *American Journal of Public Health,* 1998, 88:68–74.

Hemingway H, Kuper K, Marmot MG. Psychosocial factors in the primary and secondary prevention of coronary heart disease: an updated systematic review of prospective cohort studies. In: Yusuf S et al., eds. *Evidence-based cardiology,* 2nd ed. London, BMJ Books, 2003:181–217.

Marmot MG et al. Contribution of job control to social gradient in coronary heart disease incidence. *Lancet,* 1997, 350:235–240.

Peter R et al. and the SHEEP Study Group. Psychosocial work environment and myocardial infarction: improving risk estimation by combining two complementary job stress models in the SHEEP Study. *Journal of Epidemiology and Community Health,* 2002, 56(4):294–300.

Schnall P et al. Why the workplace and cardiovascular disease? *Occupational Medicine, State of the Art Reviews,* 2000, 15:126.

Theorell T, Karasek R. The demand-control-support model and CVD. In: Schnall PL et al., eds. *The workplace and cardiovascular disease. Occupational medicine.* Philadelphia, Hanley and Belfus Inc., 2000: 78–83.

Source of Fig. 4: Bosma H et al. Two alternative job stress models and risk of coronary heart disease. *American Journal of Public Health,* 1998, 88:68–74.

Job security increases health, well-being and job satisfaction. Higher rates of unemployment cause more illness and premature death.

What is known

Unemployment puts health at risk, and the risk is higher in regions where unemployment is widespread. Evidence from a number of countries shows that, even after allowing for other factors, unemployed people and their families suffer a substantially increased risk of premature death. The health effects of unemployment are linked to both its psychological consequences and the financial problems it brings – especially debt.

The health effects start when people first feel their jobs are threatened, even before they actually become unemployed. This shows that anxiety about insecurity is also detrimental to health. Job insecurity has been shown to increase effects on mental health (particularly anxiety and depression), self-reported ill health, heart disease and risk factors for heart disease. Because very unsatisfactory or insecure jobs can be as harmful as unemployment, merely having a job will not always protect physical and mental health: job quality is also important (Fig. 5).

During the 1990s, changes in the economies and labour markets of many industrialized countries increased feelings of job insecurity. As job insecurity continues, it acts as a chronic stressor whose effects grow with the length of exposure; it increases sickness absence and health service use.

Unemployed people and their families suffer a much higher risk of premature death.

© REUTER/POLFOTO

Policy implications

Policy should have three goals: to prevent unemployment and job insecurity; to reduce the hardship suffered by the unemployed; and to restore people to secure jobs.

- Government management of the economy to reduce the highs and lows of the business cycle can make an important contribution to job security and the reduction of unemployment.

- Limitations on working hours may also be beneficial when pursued alongside job security and satisfaction.

- To equip people for the work available, high standards of education and good retraining schemes are important.

- For those out of work, unemployment benefits set at a higher proportion of wages are likely to have a protective effect.

- Credit unions may be beneficial by reducing debts and increasing social networks.

Fig. 5. Effect of job insecurity and unemployment on health

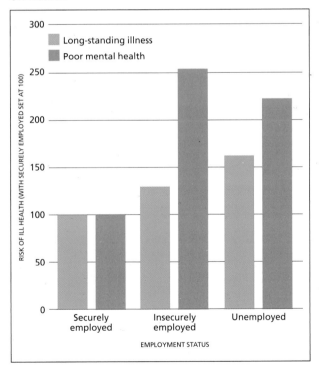

KEY SOURCES

Beale N, Nethercott S. Job-loss and family morbidity: a study of a factory closure. *Journal of the Royal College of General Practitioners,* 1985, 35:510–514.

Bethune A. Unemployment and mortality. In: Drever F, Whitehead M, eds. *Health inequalities.* London, H.M. Stationery Office, 1997.

Burchell, B. The effects of labour market position, job insecurity, and unemployment on psychological health. In: Gallie D, Marsh C, Vogler C, eds. *Social change and the experience of unemployment.* Oxford, Oxford University Press, 1994:188–212.

Ferrie J et al., eds. *Labour market changes and job insecurity: a challenge for social welfare and health promotion.* Copenhagen, WHO Regional Office for Europe, 1999 (WHO Regional Publications, European Series, No. 81) (http://www.euro.who.int/document/e66205.pdf, accessed 15 August 2003).

Iversen L et al. Unemployment and mortality in Denmark. *British Medical Journal,* 1987, 295:879–884.

Source of Fig. 5: Ferrie JE et al. Employment status and health after privatisation in white collar civil servants: prospective cohort study. *British Medical Journal,* 2001, 322:647–651.

Friendship, good social relations and strong supportive networks improve health at home, at work and in the community.

What is known

Social support and good social relations make an important contribution to health. Social support helps give people the emotional and practical resources they need. Belonging to a social network of communication and mutual obligation makes people feel cared for, loved, esteemed and valued. This has a powerful protective effect on health. Supportive relationships may also encourage healthier behaviour patterns.

Support operates on the levels both of the individual and of society. Social isolation and exclusion are associated with increased rates of premature death and poorer chances of survival after a heart attack (Fig. 6). People who get less social and emotional support from others are more likely to experience less well-being, more depression, a greater risk of pregnancy complications and higher levels of disability from chronic diseases. In addition, bad close relationships can lead to poor mental and physical health.

The amount of emotional and practical social support people get varies by social and economic status. Poverty can contribute to social exclusion and isolation.

Social cohesion – defined as the quality of social relationships and the existence of trust, mutual obligations and respect in communities or in the wider society – helps to protect people and their health. Inequality is corrosive of good social relations. Societies with high levels of income inequality tend to have less social cohesion and more violent crime. High levels of mutual support will protect health while the breakdown of social relations, sometimes following greater inequality, reduces trust and increases levels of violence. A study of a community with initially high levels of social cohesion showed low rates of coronary heart disease. When social cohesion declined, heart disease rates rose.

Policy implications

Experiments suggest that good social relations can reduce the physiological response to stress. Intervention studies have shown that providing social support can improve patient recovery rates from several different conditions. It can also improve pregnancy outcome in vulnerable groups of women.

Belonging to a social network makes people feel cared for.

© FOTOKHRONIKA/POLFOTO

Fig. 6. Level of social integration and mortality in five prospective studies

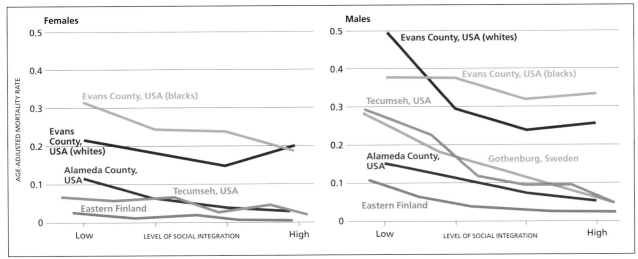

- Reducing social and economic inequalities and reducing social exclusion can lead to greater social cohesiveness and better standards of health.

- Improving the social environment in schools, in the workplace and in the community more widely, will help people feel valued and supported in more areas of their lives and will contribute to their health, especially their mental health.

- Designing facilities to encourage meeting and social interaction in communities could improve mental health.

- In all areas of both personal and institutional life, practices that cast some as socially inferior or less valuable should be avoided because they are socially divisive.

KEY SOURCES

Berkman LF, Syme SL. Social networks, host resistance and mortality: a nine year follow-up of Alameda County residents. *American Journal of Epidemiology,* 1979, 109:186–204.

Hsieh CC, Pugh MD. Poverty, income inequality, and violent crime: a meta-analysis of recent aggregate data studies. *Criminal Justice Review,* 1993, 18:182–202.

Kaplan GA et al. Social connections and mortality from all causes and from cardiovascular disease: prospective evidence from eastern Finland. *American Journal of Epidemiology,* 1988, 128: 370–380.

Kawachi I et al. A prospective study of social networks in relation to total mortality and cardiovascular disease in men in the USA. *Journal of Epidemiology and Community Health,* 1996, 50(3):245–251.

Oxman TE et al. Social support and depressive symptoms in the elderly. *American Journal of Epidemiology,* 1992, 135:356–368.

Sampson RJ, Raudenbush SW, Earls F. Neighborhoods and violent crime: a multilevel study of collective efficacy. *Science,* 1997, 277: 918–924.

Source of Fig. 6: House JS, Landis KR, Umberson D. Social relationships and health. *Science,* 1988, 241:540–545.

Individuals turn to alcohol, drugs and tobacco and suffer from their use, but use is influenced by the wider social setting.

What is known

Drug use is both a response to social breakdown and an important factor in worsening the resulting inequalities in health. It offers users a mirage of escape from adversity and stress, but only makes their problems worse.

Alcohol dependence, illicit drug use and cigarette smoking are all closely associated with markers of social and economic disadvantage (Fig. 7). In some of the transition economies of central and eastern Europe, for example, the past decade has been a time of great social upheaval. Consequently, deaths linked to alcohol use – such as accidents, violence, poisoning, injury and suicide – have risen sharply. Alcohol dependence is associated with violent death in other countries too.

The causal pathway probably runs both ways. People turn to alcohol to numb the pain of harsh economic and social conditions, and alcohol dependence leads to downward social mobility.

People turn to alcohol, drugs and tobacco to numb the pain of harsh economic and social conditions.

The irony is that, apart from a temporary release from reality, alcohol intensifies the factors that led to its use in the first place.

The same is true of tobacco. Social deprivation – whether measured by poor housing, low income, lone parenthood, unemployment or homelessness – is associated with high rates of smoking and very low rates of quitting. Smoking is a major drain on poor people's incomes and a huge cause of ill health and premature death. But nicotine offers no real relief from stress or improvement in mood.

The use of alcohol, tobacco and illicit drugs is fostered by aggressive marketing and promotion by major transnational companies and by organized crime. Their activities are a major barrier to policy initiatives to reduce use among young people; and their connivance with smuggling,

© TEIT HORNBAK/POLFOTO

Fig. 7. Socioeconomic deprivation and risk of dependence on alcohol, nicotine and drugs, Great Britain, 1993

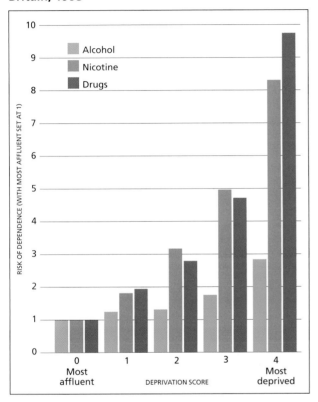

especially in the case of tobacco, has hampered efforts by governments to use price mechanisms to limit consumption.

Policy implications

- Work to deal with problems of both legal and illicit drug use needs not only to support and treat people who have developed addictive patterns of use, but also to address the patterns of social deprivation in which the problems are rooted.

- Policies need to regulate availability through pricing and licensing, and to inform people about less harmful forms of use, to use health education to reduce recruitment of young people and to provide effective treatment services for addicts.

- None of these will succeed if the social factors that breed drug use are left unchanged. Trying to shift the whole responsibility on to the user is clearly an inadequate response. This blames the victim, rather than addressing the complexities of the social circumstances that generate drug use. Effective drug policy must therefore be supported by the broad framework of social and economic policy.

KEY SOURCES

Bobak M et al. Poverty and smoking. In: Jha P, Chaloupka F, eds. *Tobacco control in developing countries.* Oxford, Oxford University Press, 2000:41–61.

Makela P, Valkonen T, Martelin T. Contribution of deaths related to alcohol use of socioeconomic variation in mortality: register based follow-up study. *British Medical Journal* 1997, 315:211–216

Marsh A, McKay S. *Poor smokers.* London, Policy Studies Institute, 1994.

Meltzer H. *Economic activity and social functioning of residents with psychiatric disorders.* London, H.M. Stationery Office, 1996 (OPCS Surveys of Psychiatric Morbidity in Great Britain, Report 6).

Ryan, M. Alcoholism and rising mortality in the Russian Federation. *British Medical Journal,* 1995, 310:646–648.

Source of Fig. 7: Wardle J et al., eds. Smoking, drinking, physical activity and screening uptake and health inequalities. In: Gordon D et al, eds. *Inequalities in health.* Bristol, The Policy Press, 1999: 213–239.

Because global market forces control the food supply, healthy food is a political issue.

What is known

A good diet and adequate food supply are central for promoting health and well-being. A shortage of food and lack of variety cause malnutrition and deficiency diseases. Excess intake (also a form of malnutrition) contributes to cardiovascular diseases, diabetes, cancer, degenerative eye diseases, obesity and dental caries. Food poverty exists side by side with food plenty. The important public health issue is the availability and cost of healthy, nutritious food (Fig. 8). Access to good, affordable food makes more difference to what people eat than health education.

Economic growth and improvements in housing and sanitation brought with them the epidemiological transition from infectious to chronic diseases – including heart disease, stroke and cancer. With it came a nutritional transition, when diets, particularly in western Europe, changed to overconsumption of energy-dense fats and sugars, producing more obesity. At the same time, obesity became more common among the poor than the rich.

World food trade is now big business. The General Agreement on Tariffs and Trade and the Common Agricultural Policy of the European Union allow global market forces to shape the food supply. International committees such as Codex Alimentarius, which determine food quality and safety standards, lack public health representatives, and food industry interests are strong. Local food production can be more sustainable, more accessible and support the local economy.

Social and economic conditions result in a social gradient in diet quality that contributes to health inequalities. The main dietary difference between social classes is the source of nutrients. In many countries, the poor tend to substitute cheaper processed foods for fresh food. High fat intakes often occur in all social groups. People on low incomes, such as young families, elderly people and the unemployed, are least able to eat well.

Dietary goals to prevent chronic diseases emphasize eating more fresh vegetables, fruits and pulses (legumes) and more minimally processed starchy foods, but less animal fat, refined sugars and salt. Over 100 expert committees have agreed on these dietary goals.

© AILEEN ROBERTSON/WHO

Local production for local consumption.

Policy implications

Local, national and international government agencies, nongovernmental organizations and the food industry should ensure:

- the integration of public health perspectives into the food system to provide affordable and nutritious fresh food for all, especially the most vulnerable;

- democratic, transparent decision-making and accountability in all food regulation matters, with participation by all stakeholders, including consumers;

- support for sustainable agriculture and food production methods that conserve natural resources and the environment;

- a stronger food culture for health, especially through school education, to foster people's knowledge of food and nutrition, cooking skills, growing food and the social value of preparing food and eating together;

- the availability of useful information about food, diet and health, especially aimed at children;

- the use of scientifically based nutrient reference values and food-based dietary guidelines to facilitate the development and implementation of policies on food and nutrition.

KEY SOURCES

Diet, nutrition and the prevention of chronic diseases. Report of a Joint WHO/FAO Expert Consultation. Geneva, World Health Organization, 2003 (WHO Technical Report Series, No. 916) (http://www.who.int/hpr/NPH/docs/who_fao_expert_report.pdf, accessed 14 August 2003)

First Action Plan for Food and Nutrition Policy [web pages]. Copenhagen, WHO Regional Office for Europe, 2000 (http://www.euro.who.int/nutrition/ActionPlan/20020729_1, accessed 14 August 2003).

Roos G et al. Disparities in vegetable and fruit consumption: European cases from the north to the south. *Public Health Nutrition*, 2001, 4:35–43

Systematic reviews in nutrition. Transforming the evidence on nutrition and health into knowledge [web site]. London, University College London, 2003 (http://www.nutritionreviews.org/, accessed 14 August 2003).

World Cancer Research Fund. *Food, nutrition and the prevention of cancer: a global perspective.* Washington, DC, American Institute for Cancer Research, 1997 (http://www.aicr.org/exreport.html, accessed 14 August 2003).

Source of Fig. 8: FAOSTAT (Food balance sheets) [database online]. Rome, Food and Agriculture Organization of the United Nations, 25 September 2003.

WHO mortality database [database online]. Geneva, World Health Organization, 25 September 2003.

Health for all database [database online]. Copenhagen, WHO Regional Office for Europe, 25 September 2003.

Fig. 8. Mortality from coronary heart disease in relation to fruit and vegetable supply in selected European countries

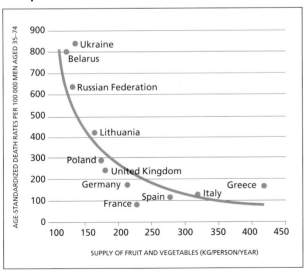

Healthy transport means less driving and more walking and cycling, backed up by better public transport.

What is known

Cycling, walking and the use of public transport promote health in four ways. They provide exercise, reduce fatal accidents, increase social contact and reduce air pollution.

Because mechanization has reduced the exercise involved in jobs and house work and added to the growing epidemic of obesity, people need to find new ways of building exercise into their lives. Transport policy can play a key role in combating sedentary lifestyles by reducing reliance on cars, increasing walking and cycling, and expanding public transport. Regular exercise protects against heart disease and, by limiting obesity, reduces the onset of diabetes. It promotes a sense of well-being and protects older people from depression.

Reducing road traffic would also reduce the toll of road deaths and serious accidents. Although accidents involving cars also injure cyclists and pedestrians, those involving cyclists injure relatively few people. Well planned urban environments, which separate cyclists and pedestrians from car traffic, increase the safety of cycling and walking.

In contrast to cars, which insulate people from each other, cycling, walking and public transport stimulate social interaction on the streets. Road traffic cuts communities in two and divides one side of the street from the other. With fewer pedestrians, streets cease to be social spaces and isolated pedestrians may fear attack. Further, suburbs that depend on cars for access isolate people without cars – particularly the young and old. Social isolation and lack of community interaction are strongly associated with poorer health.

Reduced road traffic decreases harmful pollution from exhaust. Walking and cycling make minimal use of non-renewable fuels and do not lead to global warming. They do not create disease from air pollution, make little noise and are preferable for the ecologically compact cities of the future.

Policy implications

The 21st century must see a reduction in people's dependence on cars. Despite their health-damaging

© FINN FRANDSEN/POLFOTO

Roads should give precedence to cycling.

Fig. 9. Distance travelled per person by mode of transport, Great Britain, 1985 and 2000

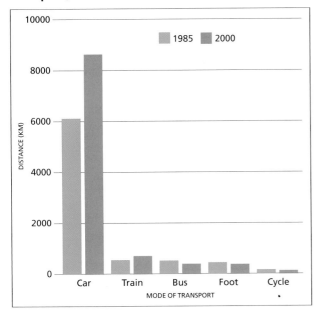

effects, however, journeys by car are rising rapidly in all European countries and journeys by foot or bicycle are falling (Fig. 9). National and local public policies must reverse these trends. Yet transport lobbies have strong vested interests. Many industries – oil, rubber, road building, car manufacturing, sales and repairs, and advertising – benefit from the use of cars.

- Roads should give precedence to cycling and walking for short journeys, especially in towns.

- Public transport should be improved for longer journeys, with regular and frequent connections for rural areas.

- Incentives need to be changed, for example, by reducing state subsidies for road building, increasing financial support for public transport, creating tax disincentives for the business use

of cars and increasing the costs and penalties of parking.

- Changes in land use are also needed, such as converting road space into green spaces, removing car parking spaces, dedicating roads to the use of pedestrians and cyclists, increasing bus and cycle lanes, and stopping the growth of low-density suburbs and out-of-town supermarkets, which increase the use of cars.

- Increasingly, the evidence suggests that building more roads encourages more car use, while traffic restrictions may, contrary to expectations, reduce congestion.

KEY SOURCES

Davies A. *Road transport and health*. London, British Medical Association, 1997.

Fletcher T, McMichael AJ, eds. *Health at the crossroads: transport policy and urban health*. New York, NY, Wiley, 1996.

Making the connections: transport and social exclusion. London, Social Exclusion Unit, Office of the Deputy Prime Minister, 2003 (http://www.socialexclusionunit.gov.uk/published.htm, accessed 14 August 2003).

McCarthy M. Transport and health. In: Marmot MG, Wilkinson R, eds. *The social determinants of health*. Oxford, Oxford University Press, 1999:132–154.

Transport, environment and health in Europe: evidence, initiatives and examples. Copenhagen, WHO Regional Office for Europe, 2001 (http://www.euro.who.int/eprise/main/who/progs/hcp/UrbanHealthTopics/20011207_1, accessed 14 August 2003).

Source of Fig. 9: Transport trends 2002: articles (Section 2: personal travel by mode). London, Department for Transport, 2002 (http://www.dft.gov.uk/stellent/groups/dft_transstats/documents/page/dft_transstats_506978.hcsp, accessed 18 September 2003).

Stress

The world health report 2001. Mental health: new understanding, new hope. Geneva, World Health Organization, 2001 (http://www.who.int/whr2001/2001/, accessed 14 August 2003).

World report on violence and health. Geneva, World Health Organization, 2002 (http://www.who.int/violence_injury_prevention/violence/world_report/wrvh1/en/, accessed 14 August 2003).

Early life

A critical link – interventions for physical growth and psychosocial development: a review. Geneva, World Health Organization, 1999 (http://whqlibdoc.who.int/hq/1999/WHO_CHS_CAH_99.3.pdf, accessed 14 August 2003).

Macroeconomics and health: investing in health for economic development. Report of the Commission on Macroeconomics and Health. Geneva, World Health Organization, 2001 (http://www3.who.int/whosis/menu.cfm?path=cmh&language=english, accessed 14 August 2003).

Social exclusion

Ziglio E et al., eds. *Health systems confront poverty.* Copenhagen, WHO Regional Office for Europe, 2003 (Public Health Case Studies, No. 1) (http://www.euro.who.int/document/e80225.pdf, accessed 14 August 2003).

Addiction

Framework Convention on Tobacco Control [web pages]. Geneva, World Health Organization, 2003 (http://www.who.int/gb/fctc/, accessed 14 August 2003).

Global status report on alcohol. Geneva, World Health Organization, 1999 (http://www.who.int/substance_abuse/pubs_alcohol.htm, accessed 14 August 2003).

The European report on tobacco control policy. Review of implementation of the Third Action Plan for a Tobacco-free Europe 1997–2001. Copenhagen, WHO Regional Office for Europe, 2002 (http://www.euro.who.int/document/tob/tobconf2002/edoc8.pdf, accessed 14 August 2003).

Food

Global strategy for infant and young child feeding [web pages]. Geneva, World Health Organization, 2002 (http://www.who.int/child-adolescent-health/NUTRITION/global_strategy.htm, accessed 15 August 2003).

Globalization, diets and noncommunicable diseases. Geneva, World Health Organization, 2002 (http://www.who.int/hpr/NPH/docs/globalization.diet.and.ncds.pdf, accessed 15 August 2003).

WHO Global Strategy on Diet, Physical Activity and Health [web pages]. Geneva, World Health Organization, 2003 (http://www.who.int/hpr/global.strategy.shtml, accessed 15 August 2003).

Transcript

A physically active life through everyday transport with a special focus on children and older people and examples and approaches from Europe. Copenhagen, WHO Regional Office for Europe, 2002 (http://www.euro.who.int/document/ e75662.pdf, accessed on 15 August 2003).

Charter on Transport, Environment and Health. Copenhagen, WHO Regional Office for Europe, 1999 (EUR/ICP/EHCO 02 02 05/9 Rev.4) (http: //www.euro.who.int/document/peh-ehp/charter_ transporte.pdf, accessed on 15 August 2003).

Dora C, Phillips M, eds. *Transport, environment and health*. Copenhagen, WHO Regional Office for Europe, 2000 (WHO Regional Publications, European Series, No. 89) (http: //www.euro.who.int/document/e72015.pdf, accessed on 15 August 2003).

Transport, Health and Environment Pan-European Programme (THE PEP) [web pages]. Geneva, United Nations Economic Commission for Europe, 2003 (http://www.unece.org/the-pep/new/en/ welcome.htm, accessed 15 August 2003).